A SHORT HISTORY
OF THE
ROMAN MASS

A SHORT HISTORY
OF THE
ROMAN MASS

By

Michael Davies

"For from the rising of the sun even to the going down, my name is great among the Gentiles, and in every place there is sacrifice, and there is offered to my name a clean oblation: for my name is great among the Gentiles, saith the Lord of Hosts."

—Malachias 1:11

TAN Books
Charlotte, North Carolina

ISBN: 0-89555-546-8

Library of Congress Catalog Card No.: 96-61302

Cover portrait of St. Pius V painted by Jacopino Del Conte (1510-1598), official portraitist in the Vatican from Pope Paul IV to Pope Clement VIII. The portrait is the property of Mario Seno, President of Una Voce Italy, and is used with his permission.

Printed and bound in the United States of America.

TAN Books
Charlotte, North Carolina
www.TANBooks.com
1997

"Our Mass goes back, without essential change, to the age when it first developed out of the oldest liturgy of all. It is still redolent of that liturgy, of the days when Ceasar ruled the world and thought he could stamp out the faith of Christ, when our fathers met together before dawn and sang a hymn to Christ as to a God. The final result of our enquiry is that, in spite of unsolved problems, in spite of later changes, there is not in Christendom another rite so venerable as ours."

—Fr. Adrian Fortescue
*The Mass: A Study of the
Roman Liturgy* (1912), p.213

"From roughly the time of St. Gregory [d. 604] we have the text of the Mass, its order and arrangement, as a sacred tradition that no one has ventured to touch except in unimportant details."

—Fr. Adrian Fortescue
*The Mass: A Study of the
Roman Liturgy* (1912), p.173

AUTHOR'S NOTE

This booklet is in large part a compilation of material from Father Adrian Fortescue's classic work, *The Mass: A Study of the Roman Liturgy* (London: Longmans, 1912). Although certain notable passages are referenced, my debt to this great priest and scholar actually goes far beyond these. I hope hereby to bring to today's readers some of the fruits of Father Fortescue's book, which is now rare and out of print. I hope also, in the near future, to publish an extensive compilation of Father Fortescue's writings on the Mass.

—Michael Davies

A SHORT HISTORY
OF THE ROMAN MASS

THE first source for the history of the Mass is obviously the account of the Last Supper in the New Testament. It was because Our Lord told us to do what He had done, in memory of Him, that Christian liturgies exist. No matter in which respects there are differences in the various Eucharistic liturgies they all obey His command to do "this," namely what He Himself had done. A definite pattern for the celebration of the Eucharist had developed within decades of the death of Our Lord, a pattern which was carried on well past the conclusion of the 1st century, and which can still be discerned clearly in the finalized Roman Mass of 1570.

THE EARLY CATHOLIC LITURGY

The earliest and most detailed account of the Eucharist is found in St. Paul's First Epistle to the Corinthians, which, of course, predates the Gospels, and was written in Ephesus between

52-55 A.D. Scholars agree that the Consecration formula used by St. Paul in *1 Corinthians*, Chapter 11, quotes verbatim from a stylized formula already in use in the Apostolic liturgy. St. Paul's account reads:

> For I have received of the Lord that which also I delivered unto you, that the Lord Jesus, the same night in which He was betrayed, took bread, and giving thanks, broke, and said: Take ye, and eat: This is My Body, which shall be delivered for you: this do for the commemoration of Me.
>
> In like manner also the chalice, after He had supped, saying: This chalice is the new testament in My Blood: this do ye, as often as you shall drink, for the commemoration of Me. For as often as you shall eat this Bread, and drink the Chalice, you shall show the death of the Lord, until He come.
>
> Therefore whosoever shall eat this Bread, or drink the Chalice of the Lord unworthily, shall be guilty of the Body and of the Blood of the Lord. (*1 Cor.* 11:23-27).

The passage is rich in doctrine. It identifies the Eucharist with the Passion. A new and permanent covenant or alliance is concluded between God and man in the Blood of Jesus. His sacrifice was mystically anticipated at the Last Supper. The Apostles, and implicitly their successors, are commanded to celebrate the Eucharist in His memory; and this remembrance is of such efficacy that it is an unceasing proclamation of His redemptive death, and renders it actually present until the day when He returns in the full glory of His Second coming. The Eucharist is the memorial of the Passion, *anamnesis* in Greek, and it commemorates the Passion by renewing it in an unbloody manner upon the altar. Finally, great purity of soul is required to take part in a rite as sacred as the offering and reception of the Body and Blood of Our Saviour.

By combining St. Paul's account with those of the four synoptic Gospels, we have the essentials of the Eucharistic liturgy in every ancient rite. Our Lord took bread, gave thanks, blessed and broke it, and gave it to His Apostles to eat; then He took a cup of wine, again gave thanks (Luke and Paul do not add this second thanksgiving), said the words of Institution (or Consecration) over it, and gave it to them to drink. We thus have the five essential elements for the Christian Eucharist: 1) Bread and wine are brought to the altar; 2) The celebrant gives thanks; 3) He takes bread, blesses it and says the words of Consecration; 4) He does the same over the wine; 5) The consecrated Bread, now having become the Body of Christ, is broken and is given to the people in Communion together with the contents of the Chalice, that is, the Precious Blood.

Our knowledge of the liturgy increases considerably in the 2nd century, and special reference must be made to the testimony of a pagan Roman—the younger Pliny (C. Plinius Caecilius, c.62-113), at that time Governor of Bithynia (modern Northwest Turkey). About the years 111-113 he writes to his master, the Emperor Trajan, to ask how he is to treat Christians. He describes what he has learned about them from Christians who had apostatized under torture. Referring to his apostate informers, he writes with satisfaction: "All have worshiped your image and the statues of the gods and have cursed Christ." Then he recounts what the apostates revealed about Christian worship:

> They assert that this is the whole of their fault or error, that they were accustomed on a certain day (*stato die*) to meet together before daybreak (*ante lucem*), and to sing a hymn alternately (*secum invicem*) to Christ as a god, and that they bound themselves by an oath (*sacramento*) not to do any crime, but only not to commit theft nor robbery nor adultery, not to break their word nor to refuse to give up a deposit. When they had done this, it was their custom to depart, but to meet again to eat food—ordinary and harmless food however. They say that they [the apostate informers] have stopped doing this after my edict which forbade private assemblies (*hetaerias*) as you commanded.[1]

The *status dies* is certainly Sunday. There are, according to Pliny, two meetings, the early one, in which they sing their hymn, and a later one, when they eat food—the Agape or Eucharist. The oath to do no wrong is probably a confusion of Pliny's mind. He would have taken it for granted that these secret meetings must involve some kind of conspirator's oath; whereas, the only obligation of which his informers could tell him was not to do wrong. Pliny's letter does not add much to our knowledge of the early liturgy, but it is worth quoting for the picture it gives, one of the first mentions of Christianity by a pagan, of the Christians meeting before daybreak and singing their hymn "to Christ as a god."

The early Christians assembled for divine worship in the house of one of their number which possessed a large dining room, a *coenaculum*, as the Vulgate puts it. This was because, as a persecuted minority, they could erect no public buildings. Our knowledge of the details of the liturgy increases from the earliest Fathers and with each succeeding century. There is a gradual and natural development. The prayers and formulas, and eventually the ceremonial actions, develop into set forms. There are varying arrangements of subsidiary parts and greater insistence on certain elements in different places will produce different liturgies, but all go back eventually to the biblical pattern. The Roman Mass is a liturgical form that we find first, not in the laws of some

medieval pope, but in the Epistles, the Acts of the
Apostles, and the Gospels.

GRADUAL DEVELOPMENT
OF CEREMONIES

Although there was considerable liturgical uniformity in the first two centuries, there was not
absolute uniformity. Liturgical books were certainly being used by the middle of the fourth century, and possibly before the end of the 3rd, but
the earliest surviving texts date from the 7th century, and musical notation was not used in the
West until the 9th century, when the melodies of
Gregorian chant were codified. The only book
known with certainty to have been used until the
4th century was the Bible, from which the lessons
were read. The *Psalms* and the Lord's Prayer were
known by heart; otherwise, the prayers were
extempore. There was little that could be
described as ceremonial in the sense that we use
the term today. Things were done as they were
done for some practical purpose. The lessons
were read in a loud voice from a convenient place
where they could be heard, and bread and wine
were brought to the altar at the appropriate
moment. Everything would evidently have been
done with the greatest possible reverence, and
gradually and naturally signs of respect emerged
and became established customs; in other words,

liturgical actions became ritualized.

The *Lavabo* or washing of hands is an evident example. In all rites the celebrant washes his hands before handling the offerings, an obvious precaution and sign of respect. St. Thomas Aquinas remarked: "We are not accustomed to handle any precious things save with clean hands; so it seems indecent that one should approach so great a sacrament with hands soiled."[2] The washing of the hands almost inevitably came to be understood as a symbol of cleansing the soul, as is the case with all ritual washing in any religion. There were originally no particular prayers mandated for the washing of hands, but it was natural that the priests at that moment should say prayers for purity, and that eventually such prayers should find their way into the liturgical books. What prayer could be more appropriate than *Psalm 25, Lavabo inter innocentes manus meas*? ("I shall wash my hands among the innocent.") Much of the ritual of the Mass grew naturally out of these purely practical actions. The only really ritual actions we find in the first two centuries are certain postures, kneeling or standing for prayer, and such ceremonies as the kiss of peace, all of which were inherited from the Jews.[3]

It is easy to understand that the order, the general outline of the service, would become constant almost unconsciously. People who do the same thing continually, naturally do it in much the same way. There was no reason for changing; to reverse the order suddenly would disturb and annoy people. The early Christians knew for instance at which moment to expect the lessons, when to receive Communion, when to stand for prayer. The fact that the catechumens were present at some part of the service, but must not see other parts, involved a certain amount of uniform order. But the prayers too, although there was as yet no idea of fixed forms, would naturally tend towards uniformity, at least in outline. Here also habit and custom would soon fix their order. The people knew when to expect the prayer for the emperor, the thanksgiving, the petitions. The dialogue form of prayer, of which we have many traces in this first period, also involves uniformity, at least in the general idea of the prayers. The people made their responses, "Amen," "Lord, have mercy," "Thanks be to God," and so on at certain points, because they knew more or less what the celebrant would say each time. In a dramatic dialogue, each side must be prepared for the other. So the order and general arrangement of the prayers would remain constant. We find in many cases the very same words being used; whole formulas, sometimes long ones, recur. This can be easily understood.

In the first place, there were many formulas that occur in the Old or New Testament that were well known in Jewish services. These were used as liturgical formulas by Christians too. Examples of such forms are: "Amen," "Alleluia," "Lord, have mercy," "Thanks be to God," "For ever and

ever," "Blessed art Thou, O Lord our God." More-
over, it will be noticed that extempore prayers
always tend to fall into stereotyped formulas. A
man who prays for the same object will soon
begin to repeat the same words. This may be
noticed in extempore preaching. The fact that all
early Christian language was saturated with Biblical forms means that it would hardly be possible for the bishop to use different words and
forms each time he prayed, even if he tried to do
so. And why should he try? So the same expres-
sions recurred over and over again in the public
prayers. A formula constantly heard would soon
be considered the right one, especially as in some
cases (the *Psalms* and Lord's Prayer) the liturgy
already contained examples of constant forms. A
younger bishop, when his turn came to celebrate,
could do no better than continue to use the very
words (as far as he remembered them) of his venerable predecessor, whose prayers the people, and
perhaps himself as deacon, had so often followed
and answered with reverent devotion.[4]

THE END OF PERSECUTION

Historical factors played a crucial role in the
manner in which the liturgy was celebrated. During times of persecution, brevity and simplicity
would be its principal characteristics, for obvious
reasons. The toleration of Christianity under Con-

stantine I and its adoption as the religion of the Empire under Theodosius I (379-395) had a dramatic effect on the development of ritual. Congregations increased in size, and benefactions for the building and furnishing of churches resulted in the enrichment of vessels and vestments. Those presenting such gifts would naturally want them to be of the richest and most beautiful nature possible. In a parallel and natural development, the liturgical rites became more elaborate, with solemn processions and stress upon the awesome nature of the rite. This elaboration of the liturgy proceeded faster and further in the East than in the West during the 4th century, but the universal change in style was initiated throughout the Christian world by the change from an illegal and private ritual into a state-supported public one.

From the 4th century onwards we have very detailed information about liturgical matters. The Fathers, such as St. Cyril of Jerusalem (d. 386), St. Athanasius (d. 373), St Basil (d. 379), St. John Chrysostom (d. 407) give us elaborate descriptions of the rites they celebrated. It is unfortunate that we know less about the earliest history of the Roman Rite than about any other. The freedom of the Church under Constantine and, roughly, the First General Council in 325 (Nicea), mark the great turning point for liturgical study. From about the 4th century, complete liturgical texts were compiled, the first *Euchologion* and Sacramentaries were drawn up for use in church. The

Euchologion is the liturgical book of the Eastern
Churches containing the Eucharistic rites, the
invariable parts of the Divine Office, and the rites
for the administration of the Sacraments and
Sacramentals, thus combining the essential parts
of the Missal, Pontifical, and *Rituale* in the
Roman Rite. By this time, the old fluid uniform
rite has crystallized into different liturgies in different places. These different liturgies all bear the
marks of their common descent and follow the
same general outline. Four parent rites can be discerned, to which all existing ancient liturgies can
be traced. Three of the parent rites are those of
the three old patriarchal cities, Rome, Alexandria
and Antioch. The general rule for liturgical usage
is that "rite followed patriarchate." The fourth
parent rite, the Gallican (early French), was an
exception to this rule as, although celebrated
within the Roman Patriarchate, it was not derived
from the rite celebrated in Rome. As this study is
concerned only with the evolution of the Roman
Rite, the liturgies of Alexandria and Antioch will
not be examined, but the Gallican Rite will, as it
had considerable influence upon the development
of the finalized Roman Rite.

THE GALLICAN RITE

The fact that until the 8th century the West did
not apply the general principle that "rite follows

patriarchate" is both anomalous and unique. That the Bishop of Rome was Patriarch of all the West is a fact not disputed by anyone, and yet the Western Churches did not follow his rite. Until the 8th century, the Roman Rite was the local rite of the city of Rome only. It was not used in northern Italy, and even the southern dioceses of the peninsula had their own liturgical use. It is usual to classify all these Western (Latin but not Roman) rites under the general name of "Gallican." This practice is justified inasmuch as they all differ from the Roman and are closely related among themselves. We know most about the Gallican rite, in the strict sense, as it was used in Gaul (ancient France). Variants are found in Spain, Britain, Italy and other countries. The generally accepted view is that the Gallican family of liturgies originated in the East, possibly in Antioch and, after being adopted in Milan during the 4th century, spread throughout the West. Milan was, at that time, the Metropolitan See of northern Italy and the second most important see in the West.

From about the 8th century, the local Roman Rite gradually spread throughout the West, displacing the Gallican liturgies, but being modified by them in the process. There are two places in Western Europe where the old Gallican liturgies are still used. The first is Toledo in Spain, the Mozarabic rite. The word "Mozarabic" refers to the mozarabes, the Christian Arabs and, strictly speaking, should only be applied to those parts of Spain which fell under Moorish rule after 711. In its present form, it is the last remnant of the old Spanish rite. From the 11th century, the Mozarabic rite was more and more driven back by that of Rome, and it seemed that it would disappear completely. In 1500 Cardinal Ximenes, the Cardinal Archbishop of Toledo who died in 1517, revised its liturgical books and founded chapters at Toledo, Salamanca and Valladolid to preserve its use, but until recently it was celebrated only in the Corpus Christi chapel in the cathedral at Toledo, founded by the Cardinal, but with Roman elements, in particular the Roman form of the words of Consecration. The Mozarabic Mass can now be used with permission in other parts of Spain but, alas, in a drastically revised version that incorporates the principles of the post-Vatican II reforms.

The city of Milan also has its own rite, commonly called Ambrosian, but there is no evidence to prove that St. Ambrose did more than compose the words of half a dozen of the hymns of the rite, which is much more Romanized than that of Toledo and includes the whole Roman Canon. The people of Milan took up arms on several occasions to resist attempts to impose the Roman Rite upon them. It was considerably modified after 1970 to bring it into line with the New Mass of Pope Paul VI.

THE ORIGINS OF THE ROMAN RITE AND ITS LITURGICAL BOOKS

By approximately the middle of the 4th century there were certainly some liturgical books. How long before that anything was written one cannot say. The first part of the liturgy to have been written appears to have been the diptychs. The word "diptych" is derived from the Greek for twice-folded. A diptych consisted of two tablets (originally covered with wax) hinged and folded together like a book. On one the names of the living for whom prayers were to be said were written, on the other the names of the dead. These names were then read out by the deacon at the appointed place in the liturgy. Their use in the East went on till far into the Middle Ages. Then the lessons were set down in a book. The old custom of reading from the Bible until the bishop made a sign to stop soon gave way to a more orderly plan of reading a certain fixed amount at each liturgy. Marginal notes were added to the Bible showing this. Then an Index giving the first and last words of the amount to be read was drawn up. Other books were read besides the Bible (lives of Saints and homilies in the Divine Office); a complete index giving references for the readings is the "Companion to the books"— *comes, liber comitis* or *comicus*. Lastly, to save trouble, the whole texts were written out as they were wanted, so we come to the (liturgical) Gospel-book *(evangelarium)*, Epistle-book *(epistolarium)*, and finally the complete Lectionary *(lectionarium)*. St. Jerome (324-420) is widely believed to have been commissioned by the pope to select the Epistles and Gospels used for each Sunday of the liturgical year, which have been used ever since in the traditional Roman Missal.[5] Meanwhile the prayers said by the celebrant and deacon were written out too.

Here we must notice an important difference between the older arrangement and the one we have now in the West. Our present books are arranged according to the service at which they are used; thus, the Missal contains all that is wanted for Mass, the Breviary contains all the Divine Office, and so on. The older system, still kept in all Eastern churches, considers not the service but the person who uses the book. One book contained all that the bishop or priest says at any service, the deacon had his book, the choir theirs, and so on. The bishop's book, from which the priest also used whatever he needed, was the Sacramentary *(Sacramentarium* or *liber sacramentorum)*. It contained only the celebrant's part of the Eucharistic liturgy—such prayers as the Canon, Collects and Prefaces, but not the Epistles and Gospels or such sung parts as the Gradual. It also contained the bishop's part in many other services—ordinations, baptism, blessings and exorcisms—in short, all sacerdotal functions. The

deacon had his book too, the *diakonikon,* but as
his function at Rome was reduced to singing the
Gospel, this book was confined to the Eastern
liturgies. And then, later, the choir had the Psalms
and responses arranged together in the *liber
antiphonarius* or *gradualis,* the *liber responsalis*
and the *psalterium;* later still there were the *hym-
narium, liber sequentialis, troponarius,* and so on,
of which in the early Middle Ages there was a
great variety.[6]

THE CANON OF THE MASS
DATES FROM THE 4TH CENTURY

Toward the end of the 4th century, St. Ambrose
of Milan, in a collection of instructions for the
newly baptized entitled *De Sacramentis,* quotes
the central part of the Canon, which is substan-
tially identical with, but somewhat shorter than,
the respective prayers of the traditional Roman
Canon. This proves beyond doubt that the core of
our traditional Canon, from the *Quam oblationem*
(the prayer before the Consecration), including
the sacrificial prayer after the Consecration, was
in existence by the end of the 4th century.

The earliest Roman Sacramentaries are the first
complete sources for the Roman Rite. These were
written in the Latin language, which had gradually replaced Greek as the language of the Roman
liturgy. Scholars differ as to the precise time when

the transition was complete, giving dates from the second half of the 3rd century up to the end of the 4th. Both languages must have been used side-by-side during a fairly long period of transition.[7] The genius of the Latin language certainly affected the ethos of the Roman Rite. Latin is naturally terse and austere when compared with the rhetorical abundance of Greek. It was a natural tendency of Latin to curtail redundant phrases, and this terseness and austerity are a noticeable mark of the Roman Mass.[8]

Of the Sacramentaries, three stand out as the earliest, the most complete, the most important in every way. These are the so-called *Leonine*, *Gelasian*, and *Gregorian Sacramentaries*, named respectively after three Popes: St. Leo (440-461), Gelasius (492-496) and St. Gregory the Great (590-604). The names imply an authorship which cannot be substantiated even in the case of St. Gregory. There is no evidence that Pope Gelasius contributed anything to the Sacramentary attributed to him; St. Leo may have composed some of the prayers in the *Leonine Sacramentary*, but this is not certain; but the *Gregorian Sacramentary* almost certainly contains some material composed by St. Gregory. The *Leonine Sacramentary*, the *Sacramentarium Leonianum*, the oldest of the three, can be found in a 7th century manuscript preserved in the Chapter Library at Verona. The Sacramentary had been preceded by what were known as *Libelli Missarum*. These were small books containing the formularies for parts of the Mass for the Church in a particular diocese or locality, but not the Canon—which was fixed—the readings, or the sung parts. They provided the intermediary between extempore celebrations and the fixed formularies of the Sacramentary. No actual examples are known to have survived, but the certainty of their existence is known through literary references and above all through the *Leonine Sacramentary*, which consists of a collection of *Libelli*. Unfortunately, the collection is not complete and lacks both the Order and the Canon of the Mass, but it contains many Mass propers, which can still be found in the Roman Missal.

The *Gelasian Sacramentary* is the oldest Roman Mass book in the proper sense of the term. It is far more complete than the Leonine and has the feasts arranged according to the ecclesiastical year. It also contains the Canon and several votive Masses. The most ancient extant manuscript dates from the 8th century and contains some Gallican material.

THE REFORM OF
ST. GREGORY THE GREAT

St. Gregory the Great became Pope in 590 and reigned until 604. His achievements during those fourteen years almost defy credibility. Prominent among the many important reforms that he undertook was that of the liturgy. His pontificate marks an epoch in the history of the Roman Mass, which in every important respect he left in the state that we still have it. He collected the Sacramentary of Gelasius into one book, leaving out much but changing little. What we now refer to as the *Gregorian Sacramentary* cannot be ascribed to the Pope himself as, apart from other evidence, it contains a Mass for his feast, but it is certainly based upon his reform of the liturgy and includes some material composed by him.

The keynote of the reform of St. Gregory was fidelity to the traditions that had been handed down. (The root meaning of the Latin word *traditio* is to hand over or hand down.) His reform consisted principally of the simplification and more orderly arrangement of the existing rite — the reduction of the variable prayers at each Mass to three (Collect, Secret and Postcommunion) and a reduction of the variations occurring at that time within the Canon, Prefaces and additional forms for the *Communicantes* and *Hanc Igitur*. These variations can still be found on a very few occasions, such as at Christmas and Easter. His principal work was certainly the definitive arrangement of the Roman Canon. The Lectionary was also given a definitive form, but subsequently was still to undergo considerable change. The Order of Mass as found in the 1570 Missal of St. Pius V (1566-1572), apart from minor additions and amplifications, corresponds very closely with the Order established by St. Gregory. It is also to this great Pope that we owe, to a large extent, the codification of the incomparable chant that bears his name.

EASTERN AND GALLICAN ADDITIONS TO THE ROMAN RITE

The Roman Mass as reformed by St. Gregory gradually spread and became predominant, not only in Italy, but also beyond the Alps. The prestige of the Roman Church, the sober nature of her liturgy, the fact that at Rome were the tombs of the Prince of the Apostles and many other martyrs, all combined to give the Roman liturgy a distinctive ethos of authenticity and authority. In addition, the absence of any great primatial see in Europe, except Toledo in Spain, and the troubled nature of the times, favored this rapid expansion. But during this expansion the Roman liturgy absorbed features of local, that is to say Gallican, traditions, which derived from an earlier period and with affinities to Eastern usages. Some of these Gallican features were eventually to find their way to Rome and to be incorporated into the Roman Mass itself.

The Sacramentary that bears the name of St. Gregory is the term used for a family of Sacramentaries which emerged after his pontificate.

The most important of the Gregorian Sacramentaries is the one referred to as *The Adrianum*. It was sent by Pope Adrian I (722-795) to Charlemagne at the request of the Emperor in 785 or 786. Charlemagne had asked for a Roman Mass book because he wished to standardize the liturgy in his Empire in accordance with the Roman usage. He was helped in this task by Alcuin, an English monk, who made up for deficiencies in the Roman Sacramentary by adding material from Gelasian sacramentaries current in Gaul, sacramentaries which contained Gallican material. Alcuin's mixed-rite sacramentary found its way back to Rome and material from it found its way into the Roman Sacramentary. It is from this Gallicanized Roman Sacramentary that the finalized Roman Missal was eventually compiled. By the 11th century, and at the latest the 12th century, this Gallicanized Roman Rite had supplanted all the pure Gallican Rites in the West, with the exception of the survival of the Mozarabic Rite at Toledo and a Romanized version of the Ambrosian Rite in Milan. The principle that "rite follows patriarchate" had finally prevailed in the West as well as the East.

The additions to the Roman Rite, some of which originated in Jerusalem and the East, as well as from Gallican rites, or via Gallican rites, form its more elaborate, decorative and symbolic parts. The pure Roman Rite was exceedingly simple, austere and plain; nothing was done except

for some reason of practical utility. Its prayers
were short and dignified, but almost too austere
when compared with the exuberant rhetoric of the
East. In our Missal we have from non-Roman
sources much of the Holy Week ritual and such
decorative and symbolic processions and blessings as those of Candlemas and Palm Sunday.
Father Adrian Fortescue writes:

> If one may venture a criticism of these
> additions from an aesthetic point of view, it
> is that they are exceedingly happy. The old
> Roman rite, in spite of its dignity and
> archaic simplicity, had the disadvantage of
> being dull. The Eastern and Gallican rites
> are too florid for our taste and too long. The
> few non-Roman elements in our Mass take
> nothing from its dignity and yet give it
> enough variety and reticent emotion to make
> it most beautiful.[9]

A SACRED HERITAGE
SINCE THE 6TH CENTURY

We have now arrived at the early Middle Ages.
From this time forward there is little to chronicle
of the nature of change in the order of the Mass
itself, which had become a sacred and inviolable
inheritance — its origin forgotten. It was popularly
believed to have been handed down unchanged

from the Apostles, or to have been written by St. Peter himself. Fr. Fortescue considers that the reign of St. Gregory the Great marks an epoch in the history of the Mass, having left the liturgy in its essentials just as we have it today. He writes:

> There is, moreover, a constant tradition that St. Gregory was the last to touch the essential part of the Mass, namely the Canon. Benedict XIV (1740-1758) says: "No pope has added to or changed the Canon since St. Gregory."[10]

Whether this is totally accurate is not a matter of great importance, and even if some very minor additions did creep in afterwards, perhaps a few Amens, the important point is that a tradition of more than a millennium certainly existed in the Roman Church that the Canon should not be changed. According to Cardinal Gasquet:

> This fact, that it has so remained unaltered during thirteen centuries, is the most speaking witness of the veneration with which it has always been regarded and of the scruple which has ever been felt at touching so sacred a heritage, coming to us from unknown antiquity.[11]

Although the rite of Mass did continue to develop after the time of St. Gregory, Fr. Fortescue explains that:

All later modifications were fitted into the old arrangement, and the most important parts were not touched. From, roughly, the time of St. Gregory we have the text of the Mass, its order and arrangement, as a sacred tradition that no one has ventured to touch except in unimportant details.[12]

Among the later additions:

The prayers said at the foot of the altar are in their present form the latest part of all. They developed out of medieval private preparations and were not formally appointed in their present state before the Missal of Pius V (1570).[13]

They were, however, widely used well before the Reformation and are found in the first printed edition of the Roman Missal (1474).

The *Gloria* was introduced gradually, at first only to be sung on feasts at bishops' Masses. It is probably Gallican. The Creed came to Rome in the 11th century. The Offertory prayers and the *Lavabo* were introduced from beyond the Alps hardly before the 14th century. The *Placeat,* Blessing and the Last Gospel were introduced gradually in the Middle Ages.[14]

These prayers almost invariably have a liturgical use stretching back centuries before their official incorporation into the Roman Rite. The *Suscipe sancte Pater* can be traced back to the prayer book of Charles the Bald (875-877).[15]

The prayers which came into the Roman Mass after the time of St. Gregory the Great were among the first to be abolished by the Protestant Reformers. They included the prayers said at the foot of the altar; the *Judica me,* with its reference to the priest going to the altar of God, and the *Confiteor* with its request for the intercession of Our Lady and the Saints were particularly unacceptable. The Offertory prayers, with their specifically sacrificial terminolgy, and the *Placeat tibi* which comes after the Communion, were totally incompatible with Protestant theology.

The fact that these prayers were incompatible with the Protestant heresy is hardly surprising, because one of the reasons which must have prompted the Church to accept them, guided by the Holy Ghost, is the exceptional clarity of their doctrinal content. This tendency for a rite to express ever more clearly what it contains is in perfect accord with the principle *lex orandi, lex credendi* ("the law of prayer is the law of belief"). This principle has been explained very clearly by Dom Fernand Cabrol, O.S.B., in the introduction to his edition of the Daily Missal:

A pope in the fifth century, in the course of a famous controversy, pronounced the following words which have been regarded, ever since, as an axiom of theology: *Legem credendi lex statuat supplicandi* ("Let the law of prayer fix the law of faith") — in other words, the liturgy of the Church is a sure guide to her teaching.

Above all else the Church prizes the integrity of the faith, of which she is the guardian: she could not therefore allow her official prayer and worship to be in contradiction with her doctrine. Thus, she has ever watched over the formulae of her liturgy with the utmost care, correcting or rejecting anything that seemed to be in any way tainted with error.

The liturgical books are, therefore, an authentic expression of the Catholic faith, and are, in fact, a source from which theologians may, in all security, draw their arguments in defense of the faith. The liturgy holds an important place among the *loci theologici* (theological sources), and in this respect its principal representative is the Missal. The latter is not, of course, a manual of Dogmatic Theology, and it is concerned with the worship of God and not with the controversial questions. It is nonetheless true that in the Missal we have a magnificent synthesis of Christian doctrine—the Holy Eucharist, Sacrifice, prayer, Christian worship, the Incarnation, and Redemption; in fact, in it all dogmas of the Faith find expression.

In the authoritative exposition of Catholic doctrine edited by Canon George Smith it is stated that:

Throughout the history of the development of the sacramental liturgy, the tendency has always been towards growth—additions and accretions, the effort to obtain a fuller, more perfect, more clearly significant symbolism.[16]

THE PROTESTANT BREAK WITH LITURGICAL TRADITION

The sound and invariable practice of the Church in the West was breached for the first time by the sixteenth-century Protestant Reformers. They broke with the tradition of the Church by the very fact of initiating a drastic reform of liturgical rites, and this would still have been the case even had their reformed liturgies been orthodox. The nature of their heresy was made clear not so much by what their rites contained as by what they omitted from the traditional books. In 1898 the Catholic bishops of the Province of Westmin-

ster published a scathing denunciation of the liturgical revolution initiated by English Reformers, a
revolution which was radically incompatible with
the principle enunciated by Canon Smith. The
Anglican claims that their services aimed at simplicity and a return to primitive usage were dealt
with in very vigorous language. The Catholic
Bishops denied the right of national or local
churches to devise their own rites.

> They must not omit or reform anything in
> those forms which immemorial tradition has
> bequeathed to us. For such an immemorial
> usage, whether or not it has in the course of
> ages incorporated superfluous accretions,
> must, in the estimation of those who believe
> in a divinely guarded visible Church, at least
> have retained whatever is necessary, so that
> in adhering rigidly to the rite handed down
> to us we can always feel secure; whereas, if
> we omit or change anything, we may per-
> haps be abandoning just that element which
> is essential. And this sound method is that
> which the Catholic Church has always fol-
> lowed . . . That in earlier times local
> churches were permitted to *add* new prayers
> and ceremonies is acknowledged . . . But
> that they were also permitted to *subtract*
> prayers and ceremonies in previous use, and
> even to remodel the existing rites in the
> most drastic manner, is a proposition for

which we know of no historical foundation, and which appears to us absolutely incredible. Hence Cranmer, in taking this unprecedented course, acted, in our opinion, with the most inconceivable rashness.[17]

THE DEVELOPMENT OF LOW MASS

The evolution of what we call Low Mass is the most important of the modifications referred to by Father Fortescue. The simplicity of the Low Mass could give rise to the impression that it is the primitive form. Nothing could be further from the truth. It is, in fact, a late abridgement. All that has been written concerning the Roman Mass so far has concerned what we would describe as the High Mass. From the beginning we read of the liturgy being celebrated with deacons and assistants and in the presence of the people who sing their part. Until the Middle Ages, Mass was not said more than once on the same day. The bishop or senior cleric celebrated, and the rest of the clergy either received Communion or concelebrated. This is still the practice in the Eastern Churches, where there is no equivalent to our Low Mass and where the original practice of one altar in each church is still kept. By the early Middle Ages in the West, every priest offered his own Mass each day, a practice which had far-reaching effects, not only upon the liturgy, but upon Church architecture and even Canon Law.

The change came about for theological reasons. Each Mass as a propitiatory sacrifice has a definite value before God; therefore, two Masses are worth twice as much as one. The custom arose of offering each Mass for a definite intention and the acceptance of a stipend for so doing. This was particularly the case where Requiem Masses were concerned. Faithful Catholics would make provision in their wills for Masses to be said for their souls and would make endowments to monastic foundations for this purpose. In the later Middle Ages, chantries were established for the specific purpose of offering requiems for a particular person, and it was the common practice of all medieval guilds to have Masses said for their deceased members. By the 9th century, the multiplication of Masses had progressed so far that many priests said Mass several times a day. (In the 13th century, action would be taken to curb the excessive multiplication of Masses, and a number of synods forbade priests to celebrate more than once a day, except on Sundays and feast days and in cases of necessity.)

The multiplication of Masses led to the building of many altars in the same church and in monasteries where many priests would celebrate at the same time on different altars. By the 9th century every large monastery was called upon to offer hundreds or even thousands of Masses each year. All these factors led to the abridged service that we call Low Mass, and it was Low Mass that caused the compilation of the Missal as we know it today.

In the earlier period, as we have seen, the books were arranged for the specific people who used them. The priest's book was the Sacramentary, containing his part of Mass and other services. He did not need to have the lessons or antiphons in his book, as he did not say them. But at a private celebration he did say these parts himself, substituting for the absent ministers and choir. Books had to be compiled containing these parts too, and the process had begun as early as the 6th century in Sacramentaries which show the beginning of this development. By the 9th century the Common Masses of Saints are often provided with Epistle, Gospel and choir's part. The 10th century saw the first attempts to compile what is known as the Perfect Missal, *Missale plenarium,* giving the text of the whole Mass.

The necessity for a truly comprehensive Perfect Missal was given a particular stimulus by the need in Rome under the pontificate of Pope Innocent III for a book that could be used by the members of the Roman curia, who had come to travel widely and frequently in undertaking their duties. It was compiled under the name of *Missale Secundum Consuetudinem Romanae Curiae,* and it spread everywhere with the final triumph of the Roman Rite. This was caused to no small extent by its adoption by the newly founded Franciscan friars, who carried it with them everywhere during their rapid spread, and, of course, eventually to the New World. From the 13th century onwards one hears no more of Sacramentaries.

Low Mass then reacted on High Mass. Originally the celebrant said or sang his part and listened, like everyone else, to the other parts—the Lessons, Gradual and so on.

Later, having become used to saying these other parts at Low Mass—in which he had to take the place of ministers and the choir himself—he began to say them at High Mass too.

Thus we have our present arrangement where the celebrant also says in a low voice at the altar whatever is sung by the ministers and choir.[18]

THE MEDIEVAL USES

Although reference has been made to the triumph of the Roman Rite, it was by no means celebrated with complete uniformity. A proliferation of local variations or "uses," such as the Sarum Rite in England, had evolved during the Middle Ages. Variations existed not simply from country to country, but from diocese to diocese. An examination of medieval Missals shows that practically every cathedral had some liturgical practices of its own, as did many religious orders, such as the Dominicans, Carmelites and Carthusians. These were merely variations of the Roman Rite and must not be confused with the Mozarabic or Ambrosian liturgies, which can be regarded justly as separate rites. Fr. Fortescue explains that

> In everything of any importance at all, Sarum (and all the other medieval rites) was simply Roman, the rite which we still use. Not only was the whole order and arrangement the same, all the important prayers were the same too. The essential element, the Canon, was word for word the same as ours. No medieval bishop dared to touch the sacred Eucharistic prayer.[19]

THE IMPORTANCE OF PRINTING

The only important development in the history of the Roman Missal between the pontificate of Innocent III in the 13th century and the publication of the Missal of St. Pius V in 1570 was the introduction of the printed Missal. The spread of printing marked a decisive stage in liturgical standardization, whether of the Roman Missal or of uses such as that of Sarum. The last Sarum Missal to be printed in England was published in London in 1557, the penultimate year of Mary Tudor's reign. The first printed edition of the Roman Missal was published in Milan in 1474 and can still be consulted there in the Ambrosian Library. It is known as *Missale Romanum Medi-*

olani. As regards the Ordinary, Canon, Proper of the time and much else, it is identical to the Missal published by St. Pius V in 1570.

Prior to the establishment of printing in Europe in the 15th century, every Missal, Bible, Pontifical, Gradual, Antiphonal or Book of Hours had been laboriously and often beautifully written by hand, usually by monks. Every monastery had its *scriptorium*. The illuminated manuscripts of these often unknown monks constitute some of the greatest masterpieces in the history of art. The destruction of countless examples of these priceless and irreplaceable treasures by the Protestant Reformers constituted a crime against civilization as well as religion, which is less well known but no less heinous than their destruction or vandalization of the churches, monasteries and cathedrals in which the liturgy so exquisitely presented in these manuscripts was celebrated. The devastation unleashed by the Reformation upon the cultural heritage of the people of England and Wales has been assessed eloquently by Professor J. J. Scarisbrick in his book *The Reformation and the English People:*

> Between 1536 and 1553 there was destruction and plunder in England of beautiful, sacred, irreplaceable things on a scale probably not witnessed before or since . . . By the end, thousands of altars had gone, countless stained glass windows, statues and wall

paintings had disappeared, numerous libraries and choirs had been dispersed. Thousands of chalices, pyxes, crosses and the like had been sold or "defaced" (smashed, presumably for easier transport) and melted down, and an untold number of precious vestments either stripped or seized.[20]

THE REFORM OF POPE ST. PIUS V

The Missal of St. Pius V was compiled and published in 1570 in obedience to the Fathers of the Council of Trent. This is the Missal that is used today whenever the Traditional Mass of the Roman Rite, commonly called the Tridentine Mass, is celebrated rather than the Mass of Pope Paul VI found in his 1970 Missal. It is the clearly expressed wish of Pope John Paul II that the Traditional Mass should be made available whenever there is a genuine desire for it on the part of the faithful.[21]

The intentions of the Fathers of the Council of Trent were well expressed by Fr. Fortescue:

The Protestant Reformers naturally played havoc with the old liturgy. It was throughout the expression of the very ideas (the Real Presence, Eucharistic Sacrifice, and so on) they rejected. So they substituted for it new communion services that expressed their principles but, of course, broke away utterly from all historic liturgical evolution. The Council of Trent (1545-1563), in opposition to the anarchy of these new services, wished the Roman Mass to be celebrated uniformly everywhere. The medieval local uses had lasted long enough. They had become very florid and exuberant; and their variety caused confusion.[22]

The first priority of the Council of Trent was to codify Catholic Eucharistic teaching. It did this in very great detail and in clear and inspiring terms. Anathema was pronounced upon anyone who rejected this teaching, and the Fathers insisted that what they had taught must remain unmodified until the End of Time:

And so this Council teaches the true and genuine doctrine about this venerable and divine sacrament of the Eucharist—the doctrine which the Catholic Church has always held and which She will hold until the end of the world, as She learned it from Christ Our Lord Himself, from His Apostles, and from the Holy Ghost, Who continually brings all truth to Her mind. The Council forbids all the faithful of Christ henceforth to believe, teach or preach anything about the most Holy Eucharist that is different from what is explained and defined in the present decree.[23]

In its eighteenth session, the Council appointed a commission to examine the Missal, to revise and restore it "according to the custom and rite of the Holy Fathers." Fr. Fortescue considers that the members of the Commission established to revise the Missal "accomplished their task very well": Their goal was not to make a new Missal, but to restore the existing one "according to the custom and rite of the holy Fathers," using for that purpose the best manuscripts and other documents.[24] He makes particular mention of the liturgical continuity which characterized the new Missal.

The Missal promulgated by St. Pius V is not simply a personal decree of the Sovereign Pontiff, but an act of the Council of Trent, even though the Council closed on December 4, 1563, before the commission had completed its task. The matter was remitted to Pope Pius IV, but he died before the work was concluded, so that it was his successor, St. Pius V, who promulgated the Missal resulting from the Council, with the Bull *Quo Primum Tempore,* July 14, 1570. Because the Missal is an act of the Council of Trent, its official title is *Missale Romanum ex decreto sacrosancti Concilii Tridentini restitutum*—"The Roman Missal Restored According to the Decrees of the Holy Council of Trent." This was the first time in the 1570 years of the Church's history that a council or pope had used legislation to specify and impose a complete rite of Mass.

NOT A NEW MASS

It would be impossible to lay too much stress upon the fact that St. Pius V did not promulgate a New Order of Mass (*Novus Ordo Missae*)! The very idea of composing a new order of Mass was and is totally alien to the whole Catholic ethos, both in the East and in the West. The Catholic tradition has been to hold fast to what has been handed down and to look upon any novelty with the utmost suspicion. Cardinal Gasquet observed that every Catholic must feel a personal love for those sacred rites when they come to him with all the authority of the centuries:

> Any rude handling of such forms must cause deep pain to those who know and use them. For they come to them from God through Christ and through the Church. But they would not have such an attraction were they not also sanctified by the piety of so many generations who have prayed in the same words and found in them steadiness in joy and consolation in sorrow.[25]

The essence of the reform of St. Pius V was, like that of St. Gregory the Great, respect for tradition; there was no question of any "rude handling" of what had been handed down. In a letter

to *The Tablet* of July 24, 1971, Father David
Knowles, Britain's most distinguished Catholic
scholar until his death in 1974, pointed out that

> The Missal of 1570 was indeed the result
> of instructions given at Trent, but it was, in
> fact, as regards the Ordinary, Canon, Proper
> of the time and much else a replica of the
> Roman Missal of 1474, which in its turn
> repeated in all essentials the practice of the
> Roman Church of the epoch of Innocent III
> [1198-1216], which itself derived from the
> usage of Gregory the Great [590-604] and
> his successors in the seventh century. In
> short, the Missal of 1570 was, in all essen-
> tials, the usage of the mainstream of
> medieval European liturgy, which included
> England and all its rites.

Writing in 1912, Father Fortescue was able to
comment with satisfaction:

> The Missal of Pius V is the one we still
> use. Later revisions are of slight importance.
> No doubt in every reform one may find
> something that one would have preferred not
> to change. Still, a just and reasonable criti-
> cism will admit that Pius V's restoration was
> on the whole eminently satisfactory. The
> standard of the commission was antiquity.
> They abolished later ornate features and

made for simplicity, yet without destroying all those picturesque elements that add poetic beauty to the severe Roman Mass. They expelled the host of long sequences that crowded Mass continually, but kept what are undoubtedly the five best; they reduced processions and elaborate, ceremonial, yet kept the really pregnant ceremonies, candles, ashes, palms and the beautiful Holy Week rites. Certainly we in the West may be very glad that we have the Roman rite in the form of Pius V's Missal.[26]

THE ANTIQUITY AND BEAUTY OF THE ROMAN MISSAL

The antiquity of the Roman Mass is a point which needs to be stressed. There is what Father Fortescue describes as a "prejudice that imagines that everything Eastern must be old." This is a mistake, and there is no existing Eastern liturgy with a history of continual use stretching back as far as that of the Roman Mass.[27] This is particularly true with regard to the traditional Roman Canon. Dom Cabrol, O.S.B., "Father" of the Modern Liturgical Movement, stresses that: "The Canon of our Roman Rite, which in its main lines was drawn up in the fourth century, is the oldest and most venerable example of all the Eucharistic prayers in use today."[28]

Fr. Louis Bouyer, one of the leaders of the pre-Vatican II Liturgical Movement, also emphasized the fact that the Roman Canon is older than any other ancient Eucharistic prayer:

> The Roman Canon, such as it is today, goes back to St. Gregory the Great. Neither in East nor West is there any Eucharistic prayer remaining in use today that can boast such antiquity. For the Roman Church to throw it overboard would be tantamount, in the eyes not only of the Orthodox, but also of the Anglicans and even Protestants having still to some extent a sense of tradition, to a denial of all claim any more to be the true Catholic Church.[29]

It is scarcely possible to exaggerate the importance of the traditional Roman Missal from any standpoint. Dr. Anton Baumstark (1872-1948), perhaps the greatest liturgical scholar of this century, expressed this well when he wrote that every worshipper taking part in this liturgy "feels himself to be at the point which links those who before him, since the very earliest days of Christianity, have offered prayer and sacrifice with those who in time to come will be offering the same prayer and the same sacrifice, long after the last fragment of his mortal remains have crumbled into dust."[30]

Those who reflect upon the nature of the mystery of the Mass will wonder how men dare to celebrate it, how a priest dares to utter the words of Consecration which renew the sacrifice of Calvary, how even the most saintly layman dares to set foot in the building where it is being offered. *Terribilis est locus iste: hic domus Dei est, et porta coeli; et vocabitur aula Dei.* ("Awesome is this place: it is the house of God, and the gate of heaven; and it shall be called the court of God.")[31]

It is natural that the Church, the steward of these holy mysteries, should clothe them with the most solemn and beautiful rites and ceremonies possible. It is equally natural that the book containing these rites should appropriate to itself some of the wonder and veneration evoked by the sacred mysteries themselves. This veneration for the traditional Missal is well expressed by Dom Cabrol:

> The Missal, being concerned directly with the Mass and the Holy Eucharist, which is the chief of the Sacraments, has the most right to our veneration, and with it the Pontifical and the Ritual, because those three in the early Church formed one volume, as we have seen when speaking of the Sacramentary. The Church herself seems to teach us by her actions the reverence in which the Missal should be held. At High Mass it is carried by the deacon in solemn procession to read from it the Gospel of the

day. He incenses it as a sign of respect, and it is kissed by a priest as containing the very word of God Himself.

In the Middle Ages every kind of art was lavished upon it. It was adorned with delicate miniatures, with the most beautifully executed writing and lettering and bound between sheets of ivory, or even silver and gold, and was studded with jewels like a precious reliquary.

The Missal has come into being gradually through the course of centuries always carefully guarded by the Church lest any error should slip into it. It is a summary of the authentic teaching of the Church, it reveals the true significance of the mystery which is accomplished in the Mass and of the prayers which the Church uses.

Dom Cabrol also pays tribute to the incomparable beauty of the Missal from the literary and aesthetic point of view. He stresses that this is not a question of "art for art's sake":

We know that truth cannot exist without beauty . . . The beauty of prayer consists in the true and sincere expression of deep sentiment. The Church has never disdained this beauty of form which follows as a consequence of truth; the great Cathedrals on which in past ages she lavished all the marvels of art stand witness to this.

The historical value of the Missal as a living link with the earliest and formative roots of Christian civilization in Europe is another point to which Dom Cabrol draws attention.

If these evidences of antiquity were merely a question of archaeology, we could not enlarge upon them here, but they have another immense importance. They prove the perpetuity of the Church and the continuity of her teaching. We have life by our tradition, but the Western Church has never confused fidelity to tradition with antiquarianism; she lives and grows with the time, ever advancing towards her goal; the liturgy of the Missal with its changes and developments throughout the centuries is a proof of this, but it proves also that the Church does not deny her past; she possesses a treasure from which she can draw the new and the old; and this is the secret of her adaptability, which is recognized even by her enemies. Though she adopts certain reforms, she never forgets her past history and guards preciously her relics of antiquity.

Here we have the explanation of the growing respect for the liturgy and of the great liturgical revival which we see in these days. What we may call the "archaisms" of the Missal are the expression of the faith of our fathers, which it is our duty to watch over and hand on to posterity.

In his book, *This Is the Mass,* Henri Daniel-Rops writes:

Therefore was it declared in the Catechism of the Council of Trent that no part of the Missal ought to be considered vain or superfluous; that not even the least of its phrases is to be thought wanting or insignificant. The shortest of its formularies, phrases which take no more than a few seconds to pronounce, form integral parts of a whole wherein are drawn together and set forth God's gift, Christ's sacrifice, and the grace which is dowered upon us. This whole conception has in view a sort of spiritual symphony in which all themes are taken as being expressed, developed, and unified under the guidance of one purpose.[32]

The beauty, the worth, the perfection of the Roman liturgy of the Mass, so universally acknowledged and admired, was described by Fr. Faber as "the most beautiful thing this side of heaven." He continues:

It came forth out of the grand mind of the Church, and lifted us out of earth and out of self, and wrapped us round in a cloud of

mystical sweetness and the sublimities of a
more than angelic liturgy, and purified us
almost without ourselves, and charmed us
with celestial charming, so that our very
senses seem to find vision, hearing, fra-
grance, taste and touch beyond what earth
can give.[33]

REVISIONS AFTER 1570

There have been revisions since the reform of
Pope St. Pius V, but until the changes which followed Vatican II, these were never of any significance. In some cases what are now cited as
"reforms" were mainly concerned with restoring
the Missal to the form codified by St. Pius V
when, largely due to the carelessness of printers,
deviations had begun to appear. This is particularly true of the "reforms" of Popes Clement VIII
set out in the Brief *Cum sanctissimum* of July 7,
1604 and of Urban VIII in the Brief *Si quid est,*
September 2, 1634. The "reforms" of these two
Popes have been used as a precedent for the
reform of Pope Paul VI, but it is only necessary
to glance through the Briefs of these popes to see
how utterly nonsensical such a comparison is.[34]

St. Pius X made a revision, not of the Mass
text but of the plainchant notation. The Vatican
Gradual of 1906 contains new, or rather restored,
forms of the chants sung by the celebrant, there-

fore to be printed in the Missal.

In 1955 Pope Pius XII authorized a rubrical revision, chiefly concerned with the calendar. In 1951 he had restored the Easter Vigil from the morning to the evening of Holy Saturday, and on November 16, 1955, he approved the Decree *Maxima redemptionis* reforming the Holy Week ceremonies. These reforms were welcomed and have been highly praised by some of the traditionalists who are implacably opposed to the reform of Pope Paul VI.

Pope John XXIII also made an extensive rubrical reform, which was promulgated on July 25, 1960 and took effect January 1, 1961. Once again, this was concerned principally with the calendar, and was incorporated into the Missal published in 1962. The only change made to the Ordinary of the Mass was the abolition of the *Confiteor* before the people's Communion. In none of the reforms which have been cited was any significant change made to the Ordinary of the Mass. It is thus unscholarly—even dishonest—to attempt to refute traditionalist criticisms of the New Mass by citing changes made in the Missal by the popes just named.

However, the unbroken tradition of East and West for over 1600 years, that the Eucharistic Liturgy should never be subjected to radical reform—although it might develop through the addition of new prayers and ceremonies—was breached in 1970 when the newly composed Missal of Pope Paul VI was published, the New

Order of Mass having been published in 1969.

OUR ANCIENT LITURGICAL HERITAGE

Regarding the Traditional Mass of the Roman Rite, the "Tridentine" Mass, Father Fortescue concludes (1912):

> Since the Council of Trent the history of the Mass is hardly anything but that of the composition and approval of new Masses [i.e., propers for new feast days, e.g., of newly canonized Saints]. The scheme and all the fundamental parts remain the same. No one has thought of touching the venerable liturgy of the Roman Mass, except by adding to it new propers.[35]

His final assessment of the Missal of St. Pius V merits careful meditation:

> There are many days still on which we say the Mass that has been said for centuries back to the days of the Leonine and Gelasian books [7th and 8th centuries]. And when they do come, the new Masses only affect the Proper. Our Canon is untouched, and all the scheme of the Mass. Our Missal is still that of Pius V. We may be very thankful that his Commission was so scrupulous to keep or restore the old Roman tradition.

Essentially, the Missal of Pius V is the Gregorian Sacramentary; that again is formed from the Gelasian book, which depends on the Leonine collection. We find the prayers of our Canon in the treatise *De Sacramentis* [of St. Ambrose, c. 340-397] and allusions to it in the IVth century. So our Mass goes back, without essential change, to the age when it first developed out of the oldest liturgy of all. It is still redolent of that liturgy, of the days when Caesar ruled the world and thought he could stamp out the faith of Christ, when our fathers met together before dawn and sang a hymn to Christ as to a God. The final result of our enquiry is that, in spite of unsolved problems, in spite of later changes, there is not in Christendom another rite so venerable as ours.[36]

Msgr. Klaus Gamber, one of the greatest liturgists of this century, asks in his book, *The Reform of the Roman Liturgy,* a very pertinent question concerning the motivation of those "experts" who devised the drastic liturgical reform of 1970—a reform which was certainly not envisaged by the bishops who voted for the generalized guidelines of the Liturgy Constitution (1963) of the Second Vatican Council.

Was all this really done because of a pastoral concern about the souls of the faithful, or did it not rather represent a radical breach with the traditional rite, to prevent the further use of traditional liturgical texts and thus make the celebration of the "Tridentine Mass" impossible—because it no longer reflected the new spirit moving through the Church?[37]

Thanks be to God, the Tridentine Mass is not simply "the most beautiful thing this side of heaven" but also the Mass that will not die. With much more reason than the faithful of Milan who refused to allow the Ambrosian Mass to be replaced by the Roman Mass, so the faithful of the Roman Rite have refused to abandon the Mass that is redolent of the liturgy "of the days when Caesar ruled the world and thought he could stamp out the faith of Christ, when our fathers met together before dawn and sang a hymn to Christ as to a God." Its renewed use is spreading throughout the world with every day that passes, and each year more and more young priests are ordained who are resolved to celebrate Mass only according to the Missal of St. Pius V, which is as certain to be the Mass of our children as it was the Mass of our fathers.

COLLECT FOR THE FEAST OF ST. PIUS V

O God, who for the overthrowing of the enemies of Thy Church, and for the restoring of the beauty of Thy worship, didst choose blessed Pius as supreme Pontiff: grant that we may so cleave unto Thy service that, overcoming all the snares of our enemies, we may rejoice in Thy eternal peace. Through Jesus Christ Thy Son Our Lord. Amen.

NOTES

The chief source for this book was Father Adrian Fortescue's classic work *The Mass: A Study of the Roman Liturgy* (London: Longmans, 1912). This work is abbreviated as TM in the notes.

1. Cited in TM, p. 16.
2. *Summa Theologica*, Part III, Q. 83, Art. 5, ad 1.
3. TM, p. 50.
4. TM, pp. 50-52.
5. TM, pp. 255 & 261.
6. TM, pp. 115-117.
7. TM, p. 126.
8. TM, p. 127.
9. TM, p. 184.
10. TM, p. 172.
11. F. Gasquet & H. Bishop, *Edward VI and the Book of Common Prayer* (London: John Hodges, 1890), p. 197.
12. TM, p. 173.
13. TM, pp. 183-184.
14. TM, p. 184.
15. TM, p. 305.
16. G. Smith, Editor, *The Teaching of the Catholic Church* (London: Burns & Oates, 1956), p. 1056.
17. The Cardinal Archbishop and Bishops of the Province of Westminster, *A Vindication of the Bull "Apostolicae Curae"* (London: Longmans, 1898), p. 42.
18. TM, pp. 185-190.
19. TM, pp. 204-205.
20. J.J. Scarisbrick, *The Reformation and the English People* (Oxford: Basil Blackwell, 1984), pp. 85 & 87.
21. Letter from Augustin Cardinal Mayer, O.S.B., President of the *Ecclesia Dei* Commission, to the Bishops of the

United States dated March 20, 1991.

22. TM, pp. 205-206.

23. H. Denzinger, *Enchiridion Symbolorum* (Editio 31), 873a.

24. TM, p. 206.

25. Gasquet & Bishop, *op. cit.*, p. 183.

26. TM, p. 208.

27. TM, p. 213n.

28. Introduction to the Cabrol edition of *The Roman Missal.*

29. Cited in Ottaviani *et al.*, *The Ottaviani Intervention: Short Critical Study of the New Order of Mass* [1969], Fr. Anthony Cekada, trans. (Rockford, Illinois: TAN, 1992), p. 57, n.1.

30. Cited in T. Klauser, *A Shorter History of the Western Liturgy* (Oxford, 1952), p. 18.

31. From the Common of the Dedication of a Church, *The Roman Missal.*

32. H. Daniel Rops, *This Is the Mass* (New York: Hawthorn Books, 1958), p. 34.

33. Cited in N. Gihr, *The Holy Sacrifice of the Mass* (St. Louis: B. Herder, 1908), p. 337.

34. The complete text of both these briefs together with the bull *Quo Primum* can be found in my book *Pope Paul's New Mass* (Angelus Press, 2818 Tracy Avenue, Kansas City, Missouri 64019, 1980).

35. TM, p. 211.

36. TM, p. 213.

37. K. Gamber, *The Reform of the Roman Liturgy* (Roman Catholic Books, P.O. Box 255, Harrison, New York 10528, 1993), p. 100.

 TAN · BOOKS

TAN Books was founded in 1967 to preserve the spiritual, intellectual and liturgical traditions of the Catholic Church. At a critical moment in history TAN kept alive the great classics of the Faith and drew many to the Church. In 2008 TAN was acquired by Saint Benedict Press. Today TAN continues its mission to a new generation of readers.

From its earliest days TAN has published a range of booklets that teach and defend the Faith. Through partnerships with organizations, apostolates, and mission-minded individuals, well over 10 million TAN booklets have been distributed.

More recently, TAN has expanded its publishing with the launch of Catholic calendars and daily planners — as well as Bibles, fiction, and multimedia products through its sister imprints Catholic Courses (catholiccourses.com) and Saint Benedict Press (saintbenedictpress.com).

Today TAN publishes over 500 titles in the areas of theology, prayer, devotions, doctrine, Church history, and the lives of the saints. TAN books are published in multiple languages and found throughout the world in schools, parishes, bookstores and homes.

For a free catalog, visit us online at
TANBooks.com

Or call us toll-free at
(800) 437-5876